To a dear
friend
Love,
Jackie
2-4-92

A VICTORIAN CELEBRATION

PARLOR CATS

BY CYNTHIA HART AND JOHN GROSSMAN
TEXT BY JOSEPHINE BANKS

WORKMAN PUBLISHING
NEW YORK

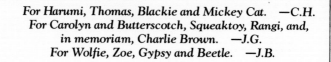

For Harumi, Thomas, Blackie and Mickey Cat. —C.H.
*For Carolyn and Butterscotch, Squeaktoy, Rangi, and,
in memoriam, Charlie Brown.* —J.G.
For Wolfie, Zoe, Gypsy and Beetle. —J.B.

Library of Congress Cataloging-in-Publication Data
Parlor Cats/by Cynthia Hart and John Grossman: text by Josephine Banks.
p. cm. ISBN: 1-56305-118-4

1. Cats—Quotations, maxims, etc.   2. Printed ephemera—Great Britain.
I. Grossman, John.   II. Banks, Josephine.   III. Title.

PN6084.C23H37 1991   820.8'036—dc20   91-50381   CIP

Workman Publishing
708 Broadway
New York, NY 10003

Printed in Japan

10 9 8 7 6 5 4 3 2 1

We offer deep and sincere thanks to Norman Karlson, Terry Ackerman, Grace and Roy Olsen, The Cat Lady Antiques (Port Washington, N.Y.) and Tender Buttons (NYC) for their extraordinarily generous loans of antique objects from their personal collections. We thank Carolyn Grossman, the proprietor of all the cat images in The John Grossman Collection of Antique Images, for their use.

We thank Steven Tex for his dedication, skill and humor through it all!

We thank Peter, Paul and Sally for being there.

For their help in so many ways, we thank Helene Weiss Winderbaum (Ilene Chazanof Antiques, NYC), Brian Albert, Benicia Berman, Mimi Vang Olsen, Starr Ockenga, Dr. Susan Siegel, Lyme Regis (NYC), Rochelle Mendle (Berkeley, Calif.), Nancy Marshall Antiques (NYC), Susan's Storeroom (San Anselmo, Calif.), Alice Kwartler (NYC), Lenore Monleon (NYC), Hoffman Gampetro Antiques (NYC), Abemayor Galleries, Inc. (NYC), Terry Rodgers Antiques (NYC); The Ephemera Society of America, (Schoharie, N.Y.), its members and its president William F. Mobley; Irene McGill, Pat Upton, Harumi Ando, Maureen Joseph; and everyone at The Gifted Line and Workman Publishing!

The photographic illustrations for this book were created by Cynthia Hart and recorded on film by Steven Tex. All the paper ephemera is from The John Grossman Collection of Antique Images.

Tabitha

CONTENTS

HOME & HEARTH

— • —

No true portrait of a Victorian household would be complete without a cat. The decorative and domestic warmth of the parlor was so frequently enhanced by the presence of these charming creatures that they are almost emblematic of the era.

The cat's strong attachment to place—stronger even than to people—suited to perfection the Victorian ideal of home and hearth. Indeed, as the intense, agitated romanticism of the *Wuthering Heights* age was swept away by the contented romantic image portrayed by the Queen as a young bride and mother, a "feline renaissance" took hold in England. Whatever Victoria did became the thing to do. And when her domestic tendencies proved to include bringing cats into the family, their place in her subjects' affections was assured. As time went on, cats came to reign supreme as the royalty of domestic animals—a role perfectly tailored to their character. Noble and independent, egotistical yet loving and loyal, they ruled with true magnanimity.

Nor was their reign limited to England. In America their popularity grew by leaps and bounds, until an article written toward the end of the nineteenth century could declare that a "cat craze" had seized the nation.

Just consider the spate of cat images from this time. Has a greater variety ever been displayed? In literature and art, on toys and artifacts—imprints of the cat were everywhere. And because of these images, made readily available to Victorian cat lovers through new, less expensive manufacturing methods and materials, we have a vivid record of the era when the cat came into its own.

THE
GOLDEN
AGE

"*It is indeed remarkable how much these animals can be taught if taken in kittenhood and treated gently. Even as soon as their eyes open, they can be made to understand many things....*"
—*Godey's Lady's Book*, May 1895

Looking at the pictures of fluffy Victorian cats with their big eyes and soft faces, lounging lazily on the hearth with colorful bows tied round their necks, one would be hard put to imagine them as anything but adored creatures. Yet, not many generations before, cats had been relegated to the barn to catch mice and to keep the foodstuffs secure from vermin. Rarely did they see the inside of a house—except perhaps the kitchen, cellar or attic.

Assigning cats to the task of pest control began in ancient Egypt, where their primary purpose was to keep graineries free from mice that would devour their contents if left unguarded. But even then, though revered for their role in preventing starvation and even elevated to godly form, cats were also beloved pets. The Victorian interest in archaeology uncovered this find. In the 1890s an article in *Godey's Lady's Book* told its readers that the cat was an acceptable and desirable household pet, no longer the stereotypical friend to lonely old ladies: "It is settled now that cats and spinsterhood have no direct connection," said the article. "A learned Egyptologist has just proclaimed the fact that ten well-beloved sacred cats were buried with an Egyptian princess, who had enjoyed the companionship of five husbands in succession. Consequently, it follows that a woman need not be an old maid to appreciate the beauties and love the virtues of her feline companions."

Cats in Roman times held a similar position of esteem, accompanying armies of

the empire to protect the stores of food. In the Middle Ages they were not so fortunate, losing their lofty status as they came to be associated with the devil's work. Women who were said to practice witchcraft reputedly kept cats as "familiars"— mysterious mediums that facilitated their evil magic.

It took centuries for cats to regain their popularity. Generally they were kept simply as utility items, thrown into the barn and otherwise ignored. Not until the 1800s, and the switch from an agricultural to an industrial economy, did the cat once again come into its own. Alive with exciting energy and explosive change, the Victorian era saw a new interest in science, in expansion and exploration, and a different way of looking at

HOUSE FRIEND

TABBY

There are Tabbies and Tortoiseshell,
Black Cats and White,

All happy and purring
from morning till night,

And though they do mischief
sometimes, which is wrong,

They're so pretty, you cannot be
cross with them long.

—Nursery rhyme

The Kittens Breakfast
A·BRUNEL.

May true friends
be around you!

the world. In this atmosphere, even the humble working cat took on a new life. Now it became a loved, domesticated pet, invited into the home as a valued member of the family.

New wealth allowed the luxury of caring for cats. And just as human food was now being processed and mass distributed (thanks to industrialization), so was food for pets. No longer did cats have to hunt or settle for scraps; special foods were made for them. All this attention, however, did not relieve them of their traditional mousing duties. With cats indoors, Victorians enjoyed a double benefit—beautiful, loving companions and leonine hunters who helped keep their beloved homes rodent-free. The mania for cleanliness dur-

The merry game of
OLD MAID

ing this period was fueled by the findings of Louis Pasteur, whose discovery that bacteria grew and that germs spread in dirty surroundings popularized the new science of hygiene. And what better symbol of hygiene than the cat, who devoted so many hours of the day to washing and preening itself?

When the natural sciences became all the rage, amateurs and professionals alike went running around the globe in search of new biological species. Thinking about animals and their relationship with humans would never be the same. Discoveries in evolution and genetics revolutionized previous concepts of creation, and animals took on a new form, a new life. Now they were God's creatures and something more—fascinating examples of the ingenuity of nature.

In *The Variation of*

MA & BABY 1ST PRIZE

AN OLD MAIDS DARLING

HAPPINESS

— · —

It's good to be a kitty,
With coat of silky fur,
And nothing else to do all day
But mew and play and purr!

You run about the garden,
And you play about the hall,
And think your sweet old mother
The dearest puss of all!

And you play with Tabby Tiptoes,
Hide and Seek in someone's hat,
Which you wouldn't dream of doing
If you were a grown-up cat!

—Nursery rhyme

To my
Valentine

Animals and Plants Under Cultivation, Charles Darwin further swayed the Victorians' interest to domestic animals rather than the exotic imports seen only in pictures or at the newly founded zoos. The domestic cats of India and South America, said Darwin, were different only in appearance from those in Europe and North America. Apart from the Manx and Persian, there was no variation in breed other than color.

Whether or not Darwin knew this observa-

tion would pique his audience's interest in cats, one will never know. But unquestionably it did—with far-reaching effects. Suddenly, the ordinary household cat had become a challenge, a subject for scrutiny and scientific investigation.

In England Harrison Weir, an artist and cat fancier, saw potential in feline breeding. "I conceived the idea that it would be well to hold Cat Shows," he later said, "so that different breeds, colours and markings might be more carefully attended to, and the domestic cat sitting in front of the fire would then possess a beauty and an attractiveness to its owner unobserved and unknown because uncultivated heretofore." His Crystal Palace show of 1871, the first of its kind, listed the permitted breeds as "Black, White and Tabby Longhairs," along with "Any Other Colour." The illustrious winner of the show was a proud Persian kitten.

Interest in new varieties spread to the United States, where cats were exhibited in dry-goods and department stores in Boston,

New York and Philadelphia. By 1895, when the first American breeds show was held at the old Madison Square Garden, cat breeding had taken a firm hold. An article published at the time named several varieties—the Angora, the Russian, the Persian, the Indian, the Abyssinian, the Siamese, the Manx and "the Wild cat"—"every one of which has a peculiarity of its own which pleases someone." A description of Angora breeding outlined the following advantages: "First is the prevention of any mixing of breeds and colors; then the kitten has individual care and attention, is fed on sweet milk and other stimulating food, has careful training, is brought up to be patient, neat and gentle. The hair is combed and braided, and the little kitten is thoroughly broken in. The health is the greatest factor, and this idea has proved to be worth many dollars. By the farming-out method, unlimited numbers can be raised and the ani-

CAT FANCY

— • —

In 1887 the National Cat Club was founded in England by Harrison Weir, who laid down the Points of Excellence for breeding. Its American counterpart, formed in Chicago in 1899, was named the Beresford Cat Club in honor of the great English cat fancier Lady Marcus Beresford.

mals can be kept perfectly pure and strong."

On the other hand, the cat lover paid dearly for the results of the breeder's diligence. An Angora could cost as much as five hundred dollars—an incredibly high sum in those days. Indeed, only the well-to-do could afford such exotic stock. Queen Victoria herself owned two Blue Persians, which she cherished as members of the immediate family. Her son Edward had several pet cats, one of whom appeared with him in autographed photos given out to the public.

Now cats were not only beautiful, practical cherished pets, they had value too! And because worth and novelty were important to Victorians, valuable cats were possessions to be desired.

Victorian life was filled not only with actual cats but also with images of cats as decoration

CHRISTMAS Greetings.
May you always have a merry part,
Keeping playful, with a kitten-heart.

A Happy New Year.

CO
PUR
1/2 OZ.
150
YDS.

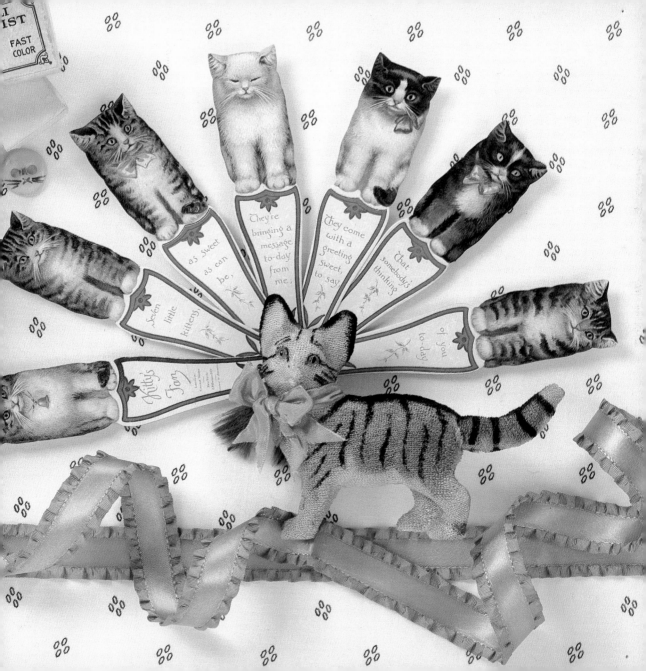

With the Season's Greetings.

C FOR CAT

C
Cat.

for the new mass-produced objects on the market. With the growth of commerce had come an influx of art and artifacts. Trade with the Orient brought paintings and prints of cats on paper— especially on fans, which in the Far East served as symbols of authority and, in some cases, royalty. From Germany and Austria came small, finely wrought porcelain and metal sculptures of cats. Germany, where printing skills went back to the invention of the press by Gutenberg, was also a source of mass-produced paper cat portraits. Emigrants to America from all over the world brought their art and skills with them, and world travelers added to the growing catalog of foreign items. All these influences were incorporated into manufacturing methods that used inexpensive materials to imitate the old expensive ones.

Cat items became the rage. The new department stores were filled with them, and the

The Tale of a Dog.

orning at eight
you'll see
a,
their family,
breakfast,—
slice of fish
ved
a china dish.

But now
and again
papa looks grave,
For oh,
the children
will not behave;
He really
cannot read
his papers,
The while
the kittens
play such capers.

SAMOA COFFEE

CATS, CATS, CATS

— · —

Suddenly, cats were everywhere—in stump work, needlework and appliqués, on paper and ceramics and metalware. Utilitarian objects such as inkwells and umbrella handles bore cat motifs. Purely decorative cat figures were abundant in metal or porcelain. Buttons were molded into cat likenesses or painted with scenes from famous cat themes, and images of cats were stamped onto spoon handles—perhaps as a by-product of the "runcible spoon" in "The Owl and the Pussy-cat".

paraphernalia of advertising reflected the demand. Colorful trade cards, one of the earliest and most effective promotion tools, portrayed cats even when the products they advertised had nothing at all to do with them.

No item that could hold a picture was missed in the mania for images made by the new technique of chromolithography, or "printing in colors." Matchboxes, cigarette containers, greeting cards, cut-out dolls and clothing, calendars, candy boxes, stationery—all invited cat decoration and all were avidly collected and treasured. Even the printed trade cards were prized as keepsakes, pasted into albums and looked at over and over again.

Wonderful prints of cats were produced by Currier & Ives, who between

1857 and 1880 put out thirty-eight large-scale lithographs of subjects including children and kittens, kittens eating and playing, a kitten sitting beside a bowl of goldfish, and the well-known Puss-in-Boots. I. Prang also used cat subjects for many famous chromolithographs and to adorn greeting cards, a Victorian innovation. Though at first unconnected with the greetings themselves, cats became a symbol of the domestic love and warmth intended in birthday wishes and in holiday messages at Christmas, Easter and Valentine's Day. The Halloween "black cat" was brought up to date, changed from a threatening symbol of superstition to a fun-filled character appropriate on a day when children bobbed for apples and roasted chestnuts by the fire.

What did the Victorian cat say about the nineteenth century? In many ways, the cat was a crazy-quilt representation of the interests and crazes of the times—an era

But the Kitten, how she starts,
Crouches, stretches, paws and darts!
First at one, and then its fellow
Just as light and just as yellow;
There are many now—
       now just one—
Now they stop and there are none;
What intenseness of desire
In her upward eye of fire!
With a tiger-leap half way
Now she meets the coming prey,
Lets it go as fast, and then
Has it in her power again;
Now she works with three or four,
Like an Indian conjurer;
Quick as he in feats of art,
Far from beyond in joy of heart…

—From "The Kitten and Falling Leaves,"
by William Wordsworth

filled with enormous energy and marked by change. Pushing full steam ahead to expand their frontiers, the Victorians felt a need to create a sense of security as protection against the unknown. They wanted to domesticate the new, to bring it into the safety and comfort of the home, to enclose and control it and make it less threatening.

> "A cat shows more of its breeding through its eyes than it does through any other feature."
>
> —Louis Wain, nineteenth-century English cat artist

What more perfect image than the cat to reflect the polar pulls created by this duality? Though driven by curiosity and vested with the courage to strike out in search of the new, the cat never fails to remember its manners. And though closely connected to untamed nature, it remains docile and loving, filled with the gentleness required of a proper Victorian.

A Happy New Year

PUSSY AT HOME

CALENDAR FOR 1907

PLAYFUL FRIENDS

NOVEMBER 1904

Sun Mon Tues Wed Thurs Fri Sat
1 2 3 4 5
6 7 8 9 10 11 12
13 14 15 16 17 18 19
20 21 22 23 24 25 26
27 28 29 30

DECEMBER 1904

Sun Mon Tues Wed Thurs Fri Sat
1 2 3
4 5 6 7 8 9 10
11 12 13 14 15 16 17
18 19 20 21 22 23 24
25 26 27 28 29 30 31

Maud Humphrey 1903

"Playing Grandma"

STRONGEST IN THE WORLD

THE EQUITABLE
LIFE ASSURANCE SOCIETY OF THE U.S.
"WORKS FOR YOU WHILE YOU PLAY"

COPYRIGHT 1903, THE GRAY LITH CO N.Y.

*"Let the little people have their live pets, by all
means, even though they do give some trouble
and some care. Girls must have something
to love, and boys something to busy
themselves about."*
—*Godey's Lady's Book*, July 1861

Recognizing that children had needs of
their own, the Victorian upbringing
saw to their pleasures as well as their
schooling. To this end, companions, toys
and books were chosen with an eye to
their capacity to entertain and instruct.

Cats were treasured as ideal playmates. Children dressed them up in
doll's clothing, put them to bed in baby
cribs, pushed them around in miniature
carriages. Treated like little people, cats
were even invited to tea parties—a Victorian invention and rage that by no means
excluded small children. Tiny tea sets
were sold by the millions. One adver-
tisement in an 1890 issue of *Ladies'
Home Journal* offered, as a premium for a

five-year subscription, a German import consisting of "23 pieces handsomely decorated in gold, Tea Pot, Sugar Bowl, Cream Pitcher, 6 Plates and 6 Cups and Saucers. Plates are 2¾ inches in diameter, other pieces in proportion." Such sets were used to entertain kitty, who wore a bib and sat at table with the other child-guests.

Not only a delightful companion for children, the cat was also a teacher of virtues, a model of decorum whose manners and behavior were ideally suited to the Victorian ideal. In 1870 *Godey's Lady's Book* advised parents that, in regard to developing the gentler side of human nature, the rearing of pets was to be recommended for the young: "The purest and sweetest satisfactions grow out of sentiments of pity, tenderness, and love, and such tend to form the noblest and most truly great char-

acters. . . . The child's play with its protegé kitten may be thus the seed of ripe fruits of tenderness and sympathy." Pets foster "the early habit of fondness for animals, regular thoughtfulness for them, and setting a value on them," *Godey's* told its readers. "The *man*, to be trustworthy and ever kind towards animals, must have grown up to it from the *boy*. Nothing is so likely to give him that excellent habit as seeing from his very birth animals taken care of and treated with great kindness by his parents, and, above all, having some pet to call his own."

Young girls, by observing the ways of mother cats, could learn the importance of one day instructing their own children in the right way to behave. Mother cats, after all, are notorious for rearing their young with a strictness not

We found this dear little kitten
Way under the entry floor;
New crept through the tiniest opening,
That must be the old cat's door;

And called me to come and get it,
'Twas as lovely as it could be,
And it really believes I'm its mother,
For its eyes are not open to see.

—From "Kitty," by Louise B. Baker

seen in other animals, for kittens untrained in survival skills will have a hard time of it in adult-hood. "The Adopted Kittens," a children's story by Agnes B. Ormsbee published in the February 1889 *Ladies' Home Journal*, illustrated the duties of feline motherhood: "So the kittens found a mother, who took good care of them, taught them how to lap milk, and to frolic; who boxed their ears when they were rough, who taught them how to wash themselves, to catch mice and know all the things that well-bred cats should, and in a year they were dignified too."

Parents were constantly encouraged to buy books for their children in the interest of entertaining and edu-

BELLING THE CAT

— · —

Taken from Aesop's fable about mice that tried to trick a cat into wearing a bell around its neck so they could hear her coming, "belling" protected canaries and other small caged birds in Victorian homes. The tinkling of the bell warned birds and owners when puss's hunting instinct got out of hand.

cating them at the same time. *Puss-in-Boots* was revived and read aloud as a lesson, as was *The Three Little Kittens* nursery rhyme. A slew of illustrated books appeared on the market for small children—who, according to the "Centre Table" gossip column, would learn far more readily if they were "in explanation of a picture." This was the time of *The Cat Who Walked Alone*, *The Owl and the Pussy-cat*, and hundreds of other classic cat stories.

The illustrations were spectacular. Besides beautifully colored standard pictures, there were ingenious three-dimensional pop-ups and overlays that could be moved to change the scene. Though still expensive, mass-produced printing and new illustration techniques allowed fairy tales to be rewritten and illustrated. Wonderful new portraits of old favorites became available to amuse and instruct the young Victorian mind.

It was almost exactly coincidental with the accession of Queen Victoria to the throne of Britain that the toy industry began to boom in the United States, spurred by newly acquired wealth and modernized factories. Soon, hundreds of toy companies were turning out millions of items—fanciful, fascinating products that reflected the vitality and variety of the era.

It was a rare class of toys that did not include cats in one form or another. The letter C in a set of alphabet building blocks was invariably represented by a cat. Some

TALES AND TAILS

— • —

Tales from Kittenland, all for you,
Told on the nursery rug,
Some with a purr! and some with a mew,
And some curled up so snug;
Some of us tabby and some of us white,
And all of us full of pranks—
For every cat has a tail, you know,
Except the cat from Manx!

—From *Tales from Kittenland*

sets, including those put out by Cran-
dall's District School Company in Chicago,
included blocks that could be built
into pictures. Others allowed children to make their own collage-pic-
tures from separate blocks that
had heads, arms and legs of
different people and animals;
these could be arranged to fash-
ion a delightful variety of chi-
merical creatures. The "Mother's
Corner" of the December 1890
Ladies' Home Journal, edited by Elizabeth
Robinson Scovie, par-
ticularly recommended

'C' was Papa's grey Cat.
Who caught a squeaky
Mouse:
She pulled him by his
twirly tail
All about the house.

—From "Nonsense Calendar,"
by Edward Lear

this type of toy because it afforded "both instruction and amusement, even for a baby."

Jigsaw puzzles (then called dissected puzzles) depicted sentimental cat scenes. Cat themes were used in card games, as well as in board games such as Kilkenny Cats. Rocking horses became rocking cats, and dollhouses boasted cats by the hearth. Cat-shaped papier-mâché toys meowed when the bellows-type base was pumped to expel air; later, these would be transformed into raised pictures mounted on heavy cardboard over a squeaker that made noise when pressed.

Rudyard Kipling, in *The Cat Who Walked Alone*, wrote that the Cat "will be kind to Babies when he is in the house, as long as they do not pull his tail too hard."

Spooners Changing Drolleries, a popular game of its time, invited children to test their imaginative powers. By rotating a disk behind a number of images with one

HALLOWE'EN

Hallowe'en Greetings.

Hallowe'en Greetings.

HALLOWEEN GREETINGS

A Jolly Hallowe'en

The Past

mith spoon so handy feeds the Cat.

The Present

or several holes, they could change the picture by substituting various body parts on a figure to make their own exotic creatures. A penny toy called a zoetrope had a circular series of pictures of the same figure, often a circus lion, in slightly different positions; when whirled around the finger, the figure seemed to walk, run, jump or perform delightfully peculiar aerobics.

Toy theaters with cardboard cutouts for characters featured cats that acted out the plots of plays written especially for them. These were often renditions of the English Christmas pantomimes that became a tradition during the nineteenth century. Based on fairy tales, many of them featured classic characters such as *Puss-in-Boots*. Although this wonderful tradition remained strictly British, the toy theaters and plays were exported abroad.

Victorians also encouraged children to make their own toys.

HEY, my kitten, my kitten,
And hey my kitten, my deary;
Such sweet little pets as these
Are neither far nor neary.

Doggy waiting for a hat, with spoon so

This silly Cat runs off from home, across the count

PUSSY'S INTRODUCTION

— • —

Dolly and I live up on the wall
Mabel and Pussy have come to call.

Pussy purrs and says "Miaow"
Dolly makes her very best bow.

For that is the proper thing to do.
Whenever a person calls on you.

—From *Told by a Cat*, a nineteenth-
century children's book

·1900·

A SUDDEN SUMMER SHOWER

To my
Valentine

An 1891 "Work Table" instructed children in doll-making and suggested a doll in the form of "an old-fashioned village school-mistress, with the head of a cat on her shoulders, in place of a human one." Shepard, Norwell of Boston advertised a kit called "Tabby Cat," which sold for 10¢ and was "printed in colors, on cloth, so that any child that can sew can make a perfect representation of a cat, life size, 13 inches high."

Thus not only real-life but decorative cats filled the quiet hours of Victorian childhood. Whether learning while at play or happily entertained at their lessons, small boys and girls on both sides of the Atlantic found themselves engaged in celebrating the cat and strengthening its renaissance as the nineteenth century drew to a close.

NINE
LIVES

"Stately, kindly, lordly friend
Condescend
Here to sit by me.
—Algernon Charles Swinburne

Cats were constant companions to Victorian writers and poets, who drew inspiration from them both in their daily lives and for their literary portraits. Edgar Allan Poe's Catalina sat on his shoulder as he worked, while Dickens' Williamina (known as William till her first litter) reportedly snuffed out the candle whenever her master became too absorbed in his reading.

John Greenleaf Whittier had the company of a cat during the winter of 1866, while he worked on *Snow-Bound*. Beatrix Potter spent her childhood among cats, which influenced her later feline heroes, and the Brontë sisters walked on the Yorkshire moors with numerous cat escorts.

Mark Twain delighted in observing the antics of his many cats, among them Apollinaire, Blatherskite and Tammany. Included in his sur-

FROM BEATRIX POTTER'S JOURNAL

— • —

"A gentleman had a favorite cat whom he taught to sit at the dinner-table, where it behaved very well. He was in the habit of putting any scraps he left on to the cat's plate. One day puss did not take his place punctually, but presently appeared with two mice, one of which he placed on his master's plate, the other on its own."

—London, Sunday, January 27, 1884

viving correspondence is a letter describing one of Tammany's kittens, who liked to be stuffed into a corner pocket of the billiard table. "He watches the game (and obstructs it) by the hour," Twain wrote, "and spoils many a shot by putting out his paw and changing the direction of a passing ball."

Harriet Beecher Stowe, a neighbor of Twain's, was also a cat-watcher. In *Juno* she wrote of "the most beautiful and best-trained cat I ever knew," and of the wise mistress who made her pet "a standing example of the virtues which may be formed in a cat by careful education."

Of course, of all the cats chronicled during this time, Edward Lear's Foss has few rivals when it comes to fame and familiarity. The subject of many drawings, including "The Heraldic Blazon," Foss also figured in Lear's self-

If one were sure your hands from Claws were free,
Your Puss-like airs might more effective be.

caricatures. So strong was the bond between the two that when Lear was forced to move from his Italian villa, he reportedly built a new one exactly like it out of concern that his dear friend would miss the old surroundings.

The cat characters of Victorian literature, following the example set by *Dame Wiggins of Lee and Her Seven Wonderful Cats* (1823), were given powers not possessed by their real-life models. The legendary Puss-in-Boots walked and schemed his way to success in a very human manner, winning his master a fortune and a princess for a wife. Lear's Pussycat was not only courted for her beauty and presented with a ring (albeit one worn by a pig at the end of his nose), but speaks to her Owl with feminine enthusiasm: "You elegant fowl! How charm-

The Owl and the Pussy-cat went to sea
In a beautiful pea-green boat,
They took some honey, and plenty of money,
Wrapped up in a five-pound note.
The Owl looked up to the stars above,
And sang to a small guitar,
"O lovely Pussy! Pussy, my love,
What a beautiful Pussy you are,
You are,
You are!
What a beautiful Pussy you are!"

Pussy said to the Owl, "You elegant fowl!
How charmingly sweet you sing!
O let us be married! too long we have tarried:
But what shall we do for a ring?"
They sailed away, for a year and a day,
To the land where the Bong-tree grows,
And there in a wood a Piggy-wig stood
With a ring at the end of his nose,
His nose,
His nose,
With a ring at the end of his nose.

—From "The Owl and the Pussy-cat," by Edward Lear

ingly sweet you sing!" Even Kipling's cat of the wet wild woods is capable of conversation, usually punctuated with his personal declaration of independence: "I am the Cat that walks by himself," he avows, " and all places are alike to me."

Perhaps the best-known of the nineteenth-century "nonsense" characters is the Cheshire Cat of Lewis Carroll's *Alice's Adventures in Wonderland*. Taken from a Welsh folk cat named for the Cheshire cheese that often cracks into "grins," this remarkable creature can vanish into thin air and return just as suddenly. It almost goes without saying that he can also speak up when Alice addresses him:

> "Cheshire Puss," she began, rather timidly, as she did not know whether it would like the name…"Would you tell me, please, which way I ought to walk from here?"

"That depends a good deal on where you want to get to," said the Cat.

"I don't much care where—" said Alice.

"Then it doesn't matter which way you walk," said the Cat.

Sly and mischievous, he responds with typical cunning when Alice objects to his abrupt disappearances:

"All right," said the Cat; and this time it vanished quite slowly, beginning with the end of the tail, and ending with the grin, which remained sometime after the rest of it had gone.

"Well! I've often seen a cat without a grin," thought Alice; "but a grin without a cat! It's the most curious thing I ever saw in all my life!"

The practice of giving cats human characteristics is centuries old, but no period in history explored and exploited the anthropomorphism of cats more than the Victorian era. To be sure, cats walked upright on their hind legs in Egyptian art, and medieval cats played musical instruments in decorations of illustrated manuscripts, but not until Grandville's nineteenth-century *Metamorphosis* and *Scenes from the Public and Private Lives of Animals* did cats take on not only physical but also character traits of human beings.

Treating cats as people, and even dressing them up in human clothes, made them more domestic—a necessity in the Victorian world. Moreover, since cats were reputed to be sexual creatures, covering their

AT WORK & PLAY

— · —

Miniature bronze figures from Vienna, often painted in naturalistic colors, showed cats engaged in familiar human pursuits— from civic duties and household chores such as laundering and sweeping, to everyday amenities and social activities.

Victorians also collected small cat figures of pewter and cast-iron, as well as enamelwork and marble.

bodies was a natural step in following the puritanical code of the day.

In addition, the Victorians developed a passionate interest in physical attributes, strengthening the connection between cats and humans. In *Miscellanea Anthropologica* (1867), for example, Groom Napier concluded that "a high mind and a low nose were never found together in the living world," an observation that applied not only to people but also to types of felines. Thus all kinds of individuals could be symbolized by cats to point up distinctions in intelligence, class and morality.

Sir Edwin Landseer, portrait painter of the Queen's animals, found cats to be suitable subjects for high art and influenced many of the animal portraits seen in Victorian homes. In general, however, cats seldom appeared

A NICE NAME FOR A CAT

— • —

In recognition of their gentleness and dignity, Victorian cats were given "people names" and even titles of respect. The family mouser, for example, was elevated to "Mrs. Lovermouse," while the erstwhile tom tabby was dubbed "Sir Thomas."

Other such cat names included:

Peter Pusskin	Priscilla Purr
Madam Satin Back	George Grimalkin
Polly Puss	Snowball Pat Paw
Tabbykin	Mrs. Tabitha Twitchit
Miss Whiskers	Mr. Kitty

in high art. In 1895 Frances E. Lanigan wrote in *Ladies' Home Journal* that "Only three of the four hunded and fifty canvases which hang in the Louvre portray the cat." She went on to speculate: "The reason for this avoidance of the cat as a subject in art is not because of its lack of charm, beauty or grace—these are admitted by everyone—but because of its difficulties. No living thing is so changeable and variable in contour, in expression and in markings . . . and none is, therefore, so difficult of portrayal." Genre painting was more characteristic of the times. To depict details of everyday life, artists simply made people into animals and animals into people. Illustrators for the popular magazines took up the fad, using cats to get their message across with sympathy or humor.

Aiming anthropomorphized cats toward adults rather than children was also a perfect forum for satire. Magazines such as *Punch* in England and *Puck* in America picked up on giving human characteristics to cats in order to poke fun at certain individuals or to reveal a truth about them. The cover of the February 18, 1880, issue of *Puck* shows Ulysses S. Grant as a tabby parlor cat with a ribbon around his neck, hanging over a goldfish bowl as he decides whether or not to run for a third term; two fish skeletons lie on a nearby table, while a live fish still swims in the bowl.

Preeminent among Victorian illustrators was Louis Wain, known as *the* cat artist of England, who pointed out the foibles of his times by using cats to reflect the character and behavior of adults.

Wain adored cats and owned many of them. In the 1880s, sitting at his wife Emily's bedside as she lay dying, he began to do sketches for her of a kitten named Peter whom she adored. It was these sketches that decided his career, which spanned six decades and at times included more than a thousand drawings a year. He took his sketch

This little kitten, Valentine, Has come to ask you to be mine.

pad with him to restaurants and other public places, always ready to "draw people in their different positions *as cats*, getting as near their human characteristics as possible." An article in *Cassall's Magazine* put it another way, calling him "the master-worker who has made cats live in a new sense—endowed them with feelings of flesh and blood, and humanized their jealousies, their loves, and their hates."

In 1890 Wain succeeded artist Harrison Weir as president of the National Cat Club, cementing his position as an expert on cats in the eyes of the public. In truth, his knowledge came simply from observing and drawing them, so that often the advice he gave was dubious at best. "If you don't want puss to go into any given place," he said in

A Happy 123 784 Christmas 80T and a bright new year to you

WHITE, BLACK & COLORS

Now, wheeling round with bootless skill,
Thy bo-peep tail provokes thee still,
And oft, beyond thy curving side,
Its jetty tip is seen to glide;
Till, from thy centre starting far,
Thou sidelong rear'st, with tail in air . . .

Doth power in measured verses dwell,
All thy vagaries wild to tell?
Ah no! the start, the jet, the bound,
The giddy scamper round and round,
With leap, and jerk, and high curvet,
And many a whirling somerset . . .

These mock the deftliest rhymester's skill,
So poor in art, though rich in will.

—From "The Kitten," by Joanne Baille

WILL YOU BE FRIENDS?

The Religious Tract Society

an 1895 interview in *Chum*, "put fresh orange peel near this place. Cats will seldom scratch up any flower at the root of which the peel is put, and I have many times known when they would not even cross a garden wall on the top of which was a continuous line of peel." (This was nowhere near as unconventional as the view held by an anonymous cat lover, quoted by Stanhope Sprigg in 1898: "I once had the impression that a cat's tendency was to travel north, and to face north as a magnet does, and that this tendency had some intimate association with the electrical strength of its fur. In brief, I looked upon a cat as a lightning conductor on a small scale."

It was in the year 1901, the last of Victoria's reign, that Wain began publishing the journal called *Wain's Annual*, devoted entirely to cats. Embellished with his own color plates, as well as with illustrations, cartoons, stories, poems and plays contributed

by others, the journal used properly domesticated subjects—from home-grown to rare, expensive breeds—and thus further popularized cats as lap pets in Victorian homes.

Thus did cats find a permanent haven in the parlor by the family hearth. Here, they served as the perfect creatures to satisfy their owners' curiosity and longings for domesticity. Above all, they were objects of love, placed foremost in their own special niche among Victorian affections.

NINE LIVES
EACH CAT MAY
SURELY MEASURE;

MAY YOURS BE
NINE TIMES FILLED
WITH PLEASURE.

—c.1875

Unless otherwise noted, all antique paper ephemera items reproduced in this book were originally printed by the nineteenth-century color process of chromolithography. Information about each item is arranged in the following order: type of item, title and/or description; size, where applicable; materials and printing method; artist, when known; lithographer, when known; date. Descriptions read clockwise, beginning at the center top of each page.

End sheets: Scrap; die cut, embossed; c1880-1900. Stock card; H.J.M., artist; c1885. Cat buttons; brass, silver, painted, fired enamel, mother-of-pearl; c1870–1930. Miniature gilt mesh cabinet with beveled-glass door; c1870. Cat with ball charm; gold with pearl; c1890. Heart locket; gold; c1880. **P.5.** New Year's card; die cut; c1895. Scrap; 5 1/2" x 8"; die cut, embossed; c1880. **P.6.** Stock calendar (calendar pad missing); 11 5/8" x 8 1/2"; die cut, embossed; c1905. **P.7.** Pin; gilt metal with faux amethyst; c1910. Lily pin; enamel on metal; c1900. Scrap; die cut, embossed; c1885. Porcelain bonneted "kitty mother and daughter" figures; German; c1880. Button; brass, purple enamel; c1900. Pin; brass grapes with faux amethyst and pearls; c1890. **P.8.** Heart locket; gold with garnets; c1890. Valentine; die cut, silvered; inscribed 1903. Hand-painted porcelain cat mewing; c1890. Bisque baby; c1880. Cat charm; gold with ruby; c1900. Miniature Eastlake chair; wood, silk; c1875. Mother cat and kitten in basket pin; gold with diamonds and rubies; c1880. **P.9.** Cat pin; gold with glass beads; c1885. Hanging fold out valentine; die cut, embossed, gilded, silk ribbon; c1900. **P.10.** "Tabitha" oil painting; English; c1850. **P.11.** Album card; embossed, gilded; c1890. Stock bookmark; imprinted "Chadwick Bros. Variety Store"; die cut, gilded; c1895. Stock album card; c1890. Scrap; die cut, embossed; c1880. Dresden candy container ornament; velvet over paperboard, embossed paper trim and ornaments, silk pouch with drawstring; Germany; c1890. Christmas card; H.J.M., artist; c1890. Scrap; die cut, embossed; c1880. Dresden candy container ornament; silk over paperboard; embossed gold foil trim, silk ribbon, paper lace trim inside; Germany; c1890.

Stock album card; c1890. Scrap; 14 1/2" x 6"; die cut, embossed; c1880. Scrap; die cut, embossed; c1880. **P.12.** Scrap; die cut, embossed; c1880–90. Oval pin; gilt with faux turquoise; c1930; Pansy pin; gold with turquoise center; c1910. **P.13.** "Egypt" pin; composition; c1940. Griffin pin; silver; c1950. Scarab pendant; silver and enamel; c1940. Egyptian cat god figurine; silver; c1990. Sewing bird; silver; c1890. Painted cat face thimble; c1940. Dresden candy container ornament; embossed, glazed paper over paperboard; embossed gold foil trim and ornaments; small chromo and embossed card applied to top; Germany; c1880. Stalking cat pin; silver-plated brass; c1920. Gunmetal-and-amber brooch; c1910. Cat in hat needlecase; pewter; c1890. Pair dressed cat quill holders; painted porcelain; c1850.

THE GOLDEN AGE

P.14. Children's book illustration; *The Three White Kittens*; T. Nelson and Sons, London and Edinburgh; c1875. Cat playing ball; hand-painted porcelain (ball is a container); c1870. Scrap; die cut, embossed; c1880. **P.15.** Button; white cat portrait on black enamel; c1860. Scrap; die cut, embossed; c1880. Pair dressed cats; porcelain; c1870. Climbing cat; porcelain (fragment); c1880.

Scrap; die cut, embossed; c1880. **P.16.** Children's book illustration; "Tabby's Tea-fight"; 10 1/2" x 9 3/4"; England; c1875. **P.17.** Stock card; die cut; c1885. Brooches; faux emerald and brass; c1920. Cat button; enamel on brass; c1910. Cat pin; brass and enamel with faux ruby; c1900. **P.18.** Cat mirror; brass with blue glass eyes; c1900. Pin, gilt with faux garnet; c1920. Cat chromolith on silk; c1880. Amber beaded frame, with tintype; c1870. Album card; illustration; c1895. Uncut scrap sheet, No. 2113; die cut, embossed; Friedberg & Silberstein; Germany; c1880. Wool flowers; c1880. **P.19.** Hand-painted fan, silk and ivory; c1900. Scrap; 8 1/2" x 5 1/2"; die cut, embossed; c1890. Cat-and-dog candlestick; bisque; 1800. Scrap; die cut, embossed; c1895. Paperboard toy; from series of Noah's Ark animals; die cut, embossed, joined by paper springs; Raphael Tuck & Sons, London; c1900. Calendar; "Frolicsome Friends"; die cut, embossed; Raphael Tuck & Sons, London; 1898. **P.20.** Inside lid cigar box label, "House Friend" (trimmed); Witsch & Schmitt, lithographers, N.Y.; c1885. Outside cigar box label, "Tabby"; Schumacher & Ettlinger, lithographers, N.Y.; c1885. Porcelain basket with cat; c1880. **P.21.** "The Kitten's Breakfast," oil painting by A. Brunel; c1887. White chalk cat; c1900. Friendship card; gilded; c1885. Pin cushion; silver and velvet; c1890. Hand-painted porcelain girl and cat (top to container); c1880. **P.22.** Hand-painted striped chalkware cat; c1870. English pottery cat; c1750. Toy foldout, "Cat Show"; die cut, embossed, accordion fold; Raphael Tuck & Sons, London; c1900. Inside lid cigar box label, "Angora" (trimmed); Schumacher & Ettlinger, lithographers, N.Y.; c1895. **P.23.** Box lid; "The Merry Game of Old Maid". Carved ivory cat chasing mouse; Japanese; c1870. Calling-card case, tortoise shell with inlaid mother-of-pearl floral motif and tiger scene; c1890. Brown polymer netsuke; c1990. Miniature leopard; painted cloth; c1910. Miniature bear rug; fur and flannel; c1910. Cat with butterfly; bronze; Japanese; c1900. **P.24.** Scrap; die cut, embossed; c1890. Postcard; A.&M.B., Germany; c1910. Puss and yellow lady slipper; porcelain; c1890. **P.25.**

Forget-me-not buttons; porcelain; c1910. White stalking cat; Royal Copenhagen porcelain; c1890. China boot; floral motifs; c1950. White cat and shoe; porcelain; French; c1870. Valentine; die cut, embossed, honeycomb paper; forget-me-not die-cut heart attached with gold cord; c1910. Scrap; die cut, embossed; c1900. **P.26.** Double-page children's book illustration with transformation center booklet; *Puss In Boots*, Pantomime Toy Book; stage scene changes as pages are turned; McLoughlin Bros, N.Y.; c1875. Cover panel from paper toy foldout, "Old Nursery Rhymes"; die cut, embossed; imprinted on reverse "Griswold's Coffee"; Raphael Tuck & Sons, London; c1900. Scrap; die cut, embossed; c1900. Foldout paper toy, "The Three Kittens"; from "Nursery Land," boxed set of 6 fairy tales; die cut, embossed; 3 stages; Raphael Tuck & Sons, London; c1895. Foldout paper toy, "Dick Whittington"; from "Nursery Land," boxed set of 6 fairy tales; die cut, embossed; 3 stages; Raphael Tuck & Sons, London; c1895. Puss-in-Boots figure; bronze; Vienna; c1890. Leather watch case; c1890. **P.27.** Paperboard toy, "C, cat"; from boxed set of 26 "Alphabetical Picture Rockers"; embossed, die cut, easel back; Samuel Gabriel Sons, N.Y.; printed in Germany; c1900. Children's book illustration, "Tom Purr"; *Pussy Cat Capers*; McLoughlin Bros., Springfield, Mass; c1910. Foldout paper toy, "Sing a Song of Sixpence"; from "Nursery Land," boxed set of 6 fairy tales; die cut, embossed; 3 stages; Raphael Tuck & Sons, London; c1895. Panels from paper toy foldout, "Old Nursery Rhymes"; die cut, embossed; Raphael Tuck & Sons, London; c1900. **P.28.** Foldout valentine; "Two's Company"; die cut, embossed, gilded, applied silk bow, 2 stages; c1910. **P.30.** Hand-painted cat face buttons; porcelain; c1910. Thread box, "Corticelli Purse Twist"; c1890. Striped embroidered and painted cloth cats; glass eyes; c1890. New Year's card; die cut, embossed; W. Hagelberg, Berlin; c1895. Transformation Christmas card; die cut, embossed; "lid" lifts to reveal kittens in box; c1895. **P.31.** Novelty fan, "Kitty's Fan"; die cut, gilded, silk tassel; Ernest Nister, London; printed in Bavaria; c1900. **P.32.** Green glazed pottery toothpick

holder; c1900. Paper toy, "C for Cat"; cover folds back to form easel back for die cut of cat; Raphael Tuck & Sons, London; c1900. Mechanical Christmas card; die cut, embossed; pull tab on right sets cats in motion; Ernest Nister, London; printed in Bavaria; inscribed 1896. **P.33.** Toy book, *The Tale of a Dog*, Ernest Nister, London; printed in Bavaria; c1895. Pop-up children's book illustration; *Peepshow Pictures*; die cut, 3 stages; Ernest Nister, London; printed in Bavaria; inscribed 1894. **P.34.** Stumpwork apple basket and kittens; New England; c1890. Scrap; die cut, embossed; c1900. **P.35.** Needlepoint Persian cat; square pillow top; c1920. Scrap; die cut, embossed; c1900. **P.36.** Cats music and art woven rug with fringe; 48" square; c1885. **P.37.** Beaded cat pouch with beaded fringe; Indian; c1905. Stock card; imprinted on reverse "The Great Inter-State Fair, Trenton, N.J."; die cut, embossed, silvered; 1892. Button; white cat portrait on black enamel; c1860. Stock card; imprinted with 1897 calendar; imprinted on reverse "J.P. Barstow & Co., dealer in stoves, ranges, and furnaces, Norwich, Conn."; die-cut edge; 1896. Christmas card set; gilded; c1890. **P.38.** Small metal cat minaudière (evening case with compartments); c1920. Large metal cat minaudière; c1920. Standing cat inkwell; bronze; Vienna; c1890. **P.39.** Cat frame; bronze; Vienna; c1880. Cat tie bar, cuff links,

tie tack; enamel on gold, with diamonds; c1900. **P.40.** Scrap; die cut, embossed; c1895. Postcard; "Humorous Cats" series; Raphael Tuck & Sons, London; postmarked 1910. Pair yellow Prattware pottery cats; c1820. **P.41.** Calendar, "Pussy at Home"; 10" x 6 3/8"; die cut, embossed; calendar printed on easel back; Raphael Tuck & Sons, London; 1907. Scrap; die cut, embossed; c1885. Stock card; imprinted New Year's greeting; die cut; J. R. Harrison; 1882. Album card; c1880.

PLAYFUL FRIENDS

P.42. Valentine; die cut; Ernest Nister, London; printed in Bavaria; envelope (not shown) postmarked 1904. Drop calendar, "Pretty Pussies"; die cut, embossed; 4 panels connected by silk ribbon; Raphael Tuck & Sons, London; 1902. Scrap; die cut, embossed; c1885. Postcard; embossed; Germany; postmarked 1911. Porcelain child's cup; c1890. Christmas card; home-trimmed with silver lace paper; L. Prang, Boston; 1890. Scrap; die cut, embossed; c1885. Postcard; A.&M.B., Germany; postmarked 1901. Child's silver spoon and fork; c1915. Porcelain cat plate; c1890. Painted porcelain flower buttons; c1900. Tiny white molded mice; c1900. **P.43.** Stock card; Raphael Tuck & Sons, London; c1895. Doll-size tea cups; c1990. Scrap; die cut, embossed; c1885-1900. Hold-to-the-light trade card; Schenck's Pulmonic Syrup; eyes appear to open when card is held to strong light; Geo. S. Harris, lithographers, Philadelphia; c1900. Scrap; die cut, embossed; c1885-1900. **P.44.** Calendar page, July, August 1904; Maud Humphrey, artist; Equitable Life Assurance Society of U.S.; Gray Litho, N.Y.; 1903. China cat with blue ball; c1940. Painted floral fan; silk with ivory; French; c1910. **P.45.** Figure of lady; bisque; c1880. **P.46.** Postcard; embossed; Germany; postmarked 1910. Silver cat salt shaker; c1910. Child's hollow spoon and food pusher; silver; c1880. Silver box with white cat; c1890. Pop-up children's book illustration; *Pretty Polly*; die cut, 3 stages; Ernest Nister, London; printed in Bavaria; inscribed 1897. Silver cat baby rattle; c1890.

Reversible trade card; Wells Richardson Lactated Food; die cut; reverse shows back view of babies; Donaldson Bros., lithographers, N.Y.; c1895. **P.47.** Child's puzzle; paper laminated to wood; 6 3/8" x 5"; c1895. Cat baby rattles; silver, ivory, mother-of-pearl; c1875. Foldout paper toy, "There was an old Woman who lived in a Shoe"; from "Nursery Land," boxed set of 6 fairy tales; die cut, embossed, 3 stages; Raphael Tuck & Sons, London; c1895. Silver baby spoon; c1900. Christmas card; H.J.M., artist; c1890. Foldout paper toy, "Nursery Playmates"; Raphael Tuck & Sons, London; c1895. Christmas card; gilt edge; Hildesheimer & Faulkner, London; c1890. Child's silver plate; c1910. **P.48.** Cloisonné enamel floral buttons; c1900. Porcelain toothpick holder; c1910. Postcard; L.M.H., artist; Meissner & Buch, Leipzig, Germany; c1905. Scrap; die cut, embossed; c1895. **P.49.** Postcard; Meissner & Buch, Leipzig, Germany; postmarked 1907. Foldout paper toy, "Evening Prayer"; die cut, embossed; Raphael Tuck & Sons, London; c1895. Scrap; die cut, embossed; c1900. Postcard; Meissner & Buch, Leipzig, Germany; postmarked 1908. Christmas card; die-cut edge; Ernest Nister, London; printed in Bavaria; c1895. Postcard; Maud Goodman, artist; Raphael Tuck & Sons, London; postmarked 1901. **P.50.** Scrap; die cut, embossed; c1900. Green-and-gold camphor glass bud vase; c1900. **P.51.** Fold-down calendars, "Friends of the Family," "Furry Friends"; Raphael Tuck & Sons, London; 1908. **P.52.** Postcard; Germany; c1905. Christmas card; die cut; W. Hagelberg, Berlin; c1895. Postcard; Germany; c1915. Postcard; Germany; c1905. Miniature red velvet chair; c1990. Miniature marble-top footed table; c1990. Miniature gilt mantel clock with china face; c1880. Scrap: Die cut, embossed; c1895. Die cut, embossed; c1900. Die cut, embossed; c1880. Album card, "Tragedy"; Helena Maguire, artist; c1895. **P.53.** Postcard; Germany; c1905. Stock trade card; imprinted "Andes Stoves and Ranges, Phillips & Clark Stove Co., Geneva, N.Y."; c1895. Postcard; Germany; c1905. Postcard; Ernest Nister, London; printed in Bavaria; postmarked 1905. New Year's card; die cut; W. Hagelberg, Berlin; c1895. **P.54.** Berlin-work

tapestry; c1875. Bronze cat with woman inside; c1920. Postcard; embossed; Paul Finkenrath, Berlin; postmarked 1907. **P.55.** Postcard; embossed; Paul Finkenrath, Berlin; c1910. Advertising calendar (trimmed); Dr. Caldwell's Syrup Pepsin; 1905. Postcard; embossed; Paul Finkenrath, Berlin; postmarked 1907. Trade card; Phillips' Digestible Cocoa; c1895. Postcard; embossed; Paul Finkenrath, Berlin; postmarked 1905. Illustration (trimmed); 14" x 11"; 1905. Postcard; embossed; Paul Finkenrath, Berlin; postmarked 1906. **P.56.** Three cat toys; printed cloth; Arnold Print Works, North Adams, Mass.; c1890. Paperboard toy, "Animals and Their Riders"; from boxed set of 10 jointed, stand-up animals with 10 interchangeable riders; die cut, embossed; Raphael Tuck & Sons, London; c1910. Cat squeak toy; painted cloth; c1900. Paperboard toy, "Rocking Animals"; from boxed set of 10 domestic and wild animals; die cut, embossed; Raphael Tuck & Sons, London; c1905. **P.57.** Paperboard toy, "Animals and Their Riders"; from boxed set of 10 jointed, stand-up animals with 10 interchangeable riders; die cut, embossed; Raphael Tuck & Sons, London; c1910. **P.58.** Postcards: Frances Brundage, artist; embossed; Samuel Gabriel, N.Y.; c1910. Frances Brundage, artist; embossed; Samuel Gabriel, N.Y.; c1910. Embossed, gilded; A. Jaeger, Germany; c1910. Ellen H. Clapsaddle, artist;

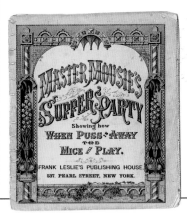

embossed, gilded; S. Garre, Germany; 1910. Samuel Smucker, artist; embossed; John Winsch, Germany; 1911. Embossed, gilded; Raphael Tuck & Sons, London; c1910. Embossed, gilded; A. Jaeger, Germany; c1910. Halloween candy containers and decorations; papier-mâché, crepe paper, wood and fabric; c1900. Black cat; molded paper; Dresden, Germany; c1900. Toy cat with fiddle and reclining cat with basket; painted cloth; c1890. **P.59.** Postcards; embossed, silvered, gilded; c1910. Ellen H. Clapsaddle, artist; embossed, gilded; S. Garre, Germany; 1909. Frances Brundage, artist; embossed; Samuel Gabriel, N.Y.; 1910. Embossed, silvered; c1910. Samuel Smucker, artist; embossed, gilded; John Winsch, Germany; 1912. Frances Brundage, artist; embossed; Samuel Gabriel, N.Y.; 1910. Embossed, gilded; Raphael Tuck & Sons, London; 1909. Haunted house, wood, glass and twigs; c1910. Fence; c1900. Witch; papier-mâché and fabric; c1910. Black cat jumping jack; wood; c1910. Black cat; chenille; c1930. Fortunetelling cards; c1890. Pipsqueak toys; papier-mâché; c1890. Dressed black cat; mechanical toy putting on pumpkin mask; papier-mâché, c1890. **P.60.** Game box, "Combination Tiddledy Winks"; 12 1/2" x 9 1/8"; paper label applied over paper-wrapped cardboard; Milton Bradley, Springfield, Mass.; c1910. Paperboard toy; from "Kittens and Puppies," boxed set of 5 kittens and 5 puppies; die cut, embossed, easel back; head pivots manually from side to side, causing change of eye expression through die-cut eye openings; tongue appears to wag; Samuel Gabriel Sons; printed in Germany; c1910. Picture blocks; paper over wood; c1910. Stand-up target board from "Combination Tiddledy Winks" game; paper over cardboard; Milton Bradley, Springfield, Mass.; c1910. Paperboard toy; die cut, embossed, easel back; head moves manually; Samuel Gabriel Sons; printed in Germany; c1910. Picture blocks; paper over wood; c1910. Game box, "Pyramid Picture Blocks"; Louis Wain, artist; paper label applied to paper-wrapped wood, hinged lid, brass clasps; 54 stacking blocks in sets of 3; c1910. Paperboard toys; die cut, embossed, easel backs; heads move manually; Samuel

Gabriel Sons; printed in Germany; c1910. **P.61.** Stacking blocks, "Picture and ABC Blocks"; from set of 7; paper over wood; McLoughlin Bros., N.Y.; c1890. Paperboard toy, "The Kit-Cat Family"; die cut, embossed; pull string on back causes seesaw motion; Raphael Tuck & Sons, London; c1910. Stand-up target board from "Combination Tiddledy Winks" game; paper over cardboard; Milton Bradley, Springfield, Mass.; c1910. Paperboard toy; from "Kittens and Puppies" boxed set of 5 kittens and 5 puppies; die cut, embossed, easel back; head pivots manually from side to side, causing change of eye expression through die-cut eye openings; tongue appears to wag; Samuel Gabriel Sons; printed in Germany; c1910. Picture blocks; from boxed set, "Pyramid Picture Blocks"; paper over wood; c1910. **P.62.** Children's book transformation illustration; *Here and There*; pull tab changes picture; Ernest Nister, London; printed in Bavaria; inscribed 1894. Children's book, *Tales from Kittenland*; 14 3/4" x 7 1/2"; paperboard cover; Raphael Tuck & Sons, London; inscribed 1903. Cat bookends; painted cast metal; Bradley and Hubbard, c1880. Shaped children's book, *Pussy's ABC*; Raphael Tuck & Sons, London; c1905. **P.63.** Children's book, *Little Folks' Fair*; 12 1/8" x 10 1/4"; Ernest Nister, London; printed in Bavaria; inscribed 1897. Cloth book, *Three Little Kittens*; c1910. Children's book pop-up illustration; *Ride a Cock Horse*; die cut; 3 stages; Ernest Nister, London; printed in Bavaria; inscribed 1896. Cat doorstop, painted white cast metal; c1890. **P.64.** Calendar illustration, "A Sudden Summer Shower"; die cut, embossed, gilded; U.S. Rubber Co.; American Litho, lithographer, N.Y.; 1910. Porcelain dish; c1910. Postcard; embossed; Germany; c1910. Calendar (calendar pad missing); die cut; brass ring for hanging; printed in Bavaria; c1900. Drop valentine; die cut, embossed; inscribed 1906. **P.65.** Advertising paper doll; J.&P. Coats' spool cotton; die cut, easel back; 1895. Postcard illustration; Raphael Tuck & Sons, London; c1905. Calendar page, September, October; Maud Humphrey, artist; Philadelphia Press; 1898. Postcard; embossed; Germany; c1910.

NINE LIVES

P.66. Shaped children's book, *Pussy Cat Capers*; 13 1/2" x 9"; die cut; McLoughlin Bros., Springfield, Mass., c1910. Postcard; "Robinhood"; Dressing Dolls' Fairy Tales series; "Oilette" (4-color process reproduction); Louis Wain, artist; Raphael Tuck & Sons, London; c1910. Child's face pins; chenille on wire, netting, beads and gilt trim; c1910. Mechanical postcard; tail rotates manually to indicate weather; Germany; c1910. Postcard; "Alladin, The Princess & The Magician"; Dressing Dolls' Fairy Tales series; "Oilette" (4-color process reproduction); Louis Wain, artist; Raphael Tuck & Sons, London; c1910. **P.67.** Trade card; Pond's Extract; c1890. Advertising paper doll; McLaughlin's Coffee; Ketterlinus, lithographer, Philadelphia; c1895. Postcards: "Little Red-Riding Hood"; Dressing Dolls' Fairy Tales series; "Oilette" (4-color process reproduction); Louis Wain, artist; Raphael Tuck & Sons, London; c1910. Christmas; postmarked 1905. Ernest Nister, London; printed in Bavaria; c1905. Louis Wain, artist; Germany; postmarked 1906. Cat with umbrella; porcelain; Louis Wain; c1890. Advertising paper doll; McLaughlin's Coffee;

Ketterlinus, lithographer, Philadelphia; c1895. Uncut scrap sheet; die cut, embossed; c1890. Postcards: Embossed; Germany; c1910. International Art Publishing, N.Y.; printed in Germany; c1905. Louis Wain, artist; handwritten inscriptions; Raphael Tuck & Sons, London; printed in Saxony; postmarked 1905. **P.68.** Uncut scrap sheet; die cut, embossed; W. Hagelberg, London and Berlin; c1890. White cat on gold ball; c1920. Assorted buttons; c1880–1910. Scrap; die cut, embossed; c1890. **P.69.** Hidden name card; die-cut edge; applied scrap lifts to reveal name, die cut, embossed; c1890. **P.70.** Stock card set; imprinted "Ozone Soap"; Fairchild & Shelton, manufacturers; © A.M. Smith, 1882. Paper doll; c1885. Snappy dress fasteners, card and box; c1880. Buttons (pair); painted paper, c1860. Household tacks box; c1870. Trade card; Baldwin Cats-Up, K.K.&F.B. Thurber & Co.; Forbes, lithographer, Boston and N.Y., c1890. Trade card, "Pet of the Household"; B.T. Babbitt's 1776 Soap Powder; Donaldson Bros., lithographers; c1890. Stock shaped card; imprinted "John A. Ackerman, Boot and Shoe Dealer, Pottsville, Pa."; c1885. **P.71.** Stock shaped card; imprinted "John A. Ackerman, Boot and Shoe Dealer, Pottsville, Pa."; c1885. Cat-and-ball match-strike; pewter and brass; c1940. Advertising window card; Pet Cigarettes; Allen & Ginter, manufacturers; Louis C. Wagner, lithographer, N.Y.; c1895. Trade cards: Vanderbilts' Fine Shoes; c1880. J.&P. Coats' Spool Cotton; Forbes, lithographer, Boston; c1885. Geneva Hand Fluter, Kane, manufacturers, Geneva, Ill.; Shover & Saroneville, lithographers, Chicago; c1880. Shaped stand-up trade card; back legs form easel; Globe Polish; Raimes, N.Y.; c1900. Trade card; Kerr's Thread, Kerr, E. Newark, N.J.; c1880. Stock shaped trade card; imprinted "Bogue's Soap, C.B. Bogue, New York"; Hughes & Johnson, lithographers, Chicago; c1890. **P.72.** Molded filigree bracelet; brass; c1940. Children's book illustration, "Tabby's Tea-Fight"; England; c1775. Christmas card; S. Hildesheimer, London; c1885. Sculpture, cast-bronze cat on base; E. Fremiet; c1850. Stock card; imprinted "Wilde's Clothing House, Chicago, Ill."; c1885. Children's book illustration, "Master Mousies' Supper Party"; Frank Leslie's Publishing House,

N.Y.; c1875. Comic valentine; inscribed 1891. Sepiatone child's portrait with cat in gilt frame; "The First Attachment"; c1860. **P.73.** Small porcelain dish; c1900. "Cat & Fiddle" dish; brass; c1940. Dresden ornaments; gold and silver foil over embossed cardboard; Germany; c1880–1910. Cat-and-mouse brass candlestick; Chinese; c1910. Stock card; imprinted "Wilde's Clothing House, Chicago, Ill."; c1885. Oval gold pin; c1890. **P.74.** Cigar labels: Top brand, "Tom & Dick"; die cut, embossed, gilded; George Schlegel, lithographer, N.Y.; c1910. Trim, "Me-Ow"; George Schlegel, lithographer, N.Y.; c1920. Back flap, outside end, cigar band, "Our Kitties"; die cut, embossed, gilded; c1910. Scrap; die cut, embossed; c1915. Cigar labels: Sample inside lid, "Tommie"; No. 1742; Johns, Cleveland; c1885. Outside end, "Me-Ow"; George Schlegel, lithographer, N.Y.; c1920. Outside end, "Night Clerk"; George Schlegel, lithographer, N.Y.; c1910. Trim, "C.A. Tripple's C.A.T."; George Schlegel, lithographer, N.Y.; c1905. Outside end, "Two Toms"; embossed, gilded; c1910. Sample inside lid, ("Red Stocking"); Witsch & Schmitt, lithographers, N.Y.; c1885. Outside end, "Tom & Jerry"; c1885. Price flap, outside end, "Tabby"; George Schlegel, lithographer, N.Y.; c1920. Sample inside lid, "Catchy"; No. 5917; embossed; O.L. Schwencke, lithographer, N.Y.; c1890. **P.75.** Cigar labels: Trim, "Me-Ow"; George Schlegel, lithographer, N.Y.; c1920. Caution notice, C.A. Tripple's C.A.T.; gilded; George Schlegel, lithographer, N.Y.; 1905. Outside end, "White Cat"; embossed, gilded; George Schlegel, lithographer, N.Y.; 1905. Inside lid proof, "Pussy White"; 4 colors plus gold; American Colortype; Clifton, N.J.; c1910. Box, "Guardian O.&S."; c1871. Trim, "C.A. Tripple's C.A.T."; Black-and-white spotted cat; porcelain; c1990. Match-safe; silver and bone; c1900. George Schlegel, lithographer, N.Y.; c1905. Scrap; die cut, embossed; c1885. Cigar labels: trim, back flap, "Night Clerk"; George Schlegel, lithographer; N.Y.; c1910. Scrap; die cut, embossed; c1900. Cigar labels: Trim, "C.A. Tripple's C.A.T."; George Schlegel, lithographer; N.Y.; c1905. Inside lid, "Peebles Cat Tails"; embossed, gilded; George Schlegel, lithographer; N.Y.; c1900. Top brand, "Tom's Den"; die cut, em-

bossed, gilded; c1910. Cigar band, "Our Kitties"; die cut, embossed, gilded; c1910. Cigar band, "White Cat"; die cut, embossed, gilded; George Schlegel, lithographer; N.Y.; 1943. Black cat on red cushion; porcelain; Rockingham; c1830. **P.76.** Children's book illustration, "Tabby's Tea-Fight"; England; c1875. Theatrical inkwell; cast metal; dated, c1897. Pin cushion; paper and cloth; c1840. Cat inkwell; cast metal; c1890. **P.77.** Cat inkwell; cast metal with glass eyes; c1880. Whieldon porcelain cat figures; c1750. **P.78.** Mouse; bronze; Vienna; c1880. Cats with dog at table; painted bronze; Vienna; c1890. Mother and kitten; painted bronze; Vienna; c1880. **P.79.** Cats lighting streetlight; painted bronze; c1910. Kissing cats; painted bronze; c1890. **P.80.** Postcard; Ernest Nister, London; printed in Bavaria; c1900. Scrap; die cut, embossed; c1905. Postcards: Pittius, Germany; c1910. Ernest Nister, London; printed in Bavaria; postmarked 1908. Ernest Nister, London; printed in Bavaria; postmarked 1908. Valentine card; die cut, embossed; c1910. Postcard; Ernest Nister, London; printed in Bavaria; c1908. Blue faux jewel buttons; c1940. Mechanical valentine; gilded; pull-tab extends arms and legs; Ernest Nister, London; printed in Bavaria; c1900. Cat figure and box, hand-painted porcelain; c1880. **P.81.** Postcard; embossed; EAS, Germany; postmarked 1909. Standing cat figure with green eyes; painted porcelain; c1880. Scrap; die cut, embossed; c1885. Postcards: Embossed; c1910. Theo. Stroefer's Kunstverlag, Nurnberg; postmarked 1901. Ernest Nister; London; printed in Bavaria; postmarked 1903. **P.82.** Cat inkwells; carved wood with glass eyes; c1880–90. Pens; gold, inlaid wood, brass and mosaic; c1880–90.

Valentines; embossed; c1890. Postcard; Germany; c1910. **P.83.** Album card; H.D., artist; die cut; hand-painted inscription; Hildesheimer & Faulkner, London; c1890. Trade card; J.&P. Coats' Best Six Cord Thread; Bufford, lithographer; c1885. Valentine; die cut; Ernest Nister, London; printed in Bavaria; c1895. **P.84.** New Year's card; Ernest Nister; London; printed in Bavaria; c1895. Scrap; die cut; embossed; c1880. Scrap; die cut, embossed; c1890. Scrap; 9 1/2" x 3 5/8"; die cut, embossed; c1885. Magazine illustration, "Will You Be Friends"; Religious Tract Society; c1875. Stock card; Major Knapp, lithographer, N.Y.; 1885. **P.85.** Fairy flower pins; silver; 1890–1900. Postcard; c1910. Shaped toy booklet, "Miss Kitty"; c1885. Miniature cats and dogs; hand-painted porcelain; c1890. Stock card; imprinted "Nellie Allen, Milliner, Quincy, Mich."; c1885. Stock calendar; imprinted "Hollingsworth & Laipply, Milford, Nebraska"; die cut, embossed; Germany; c1910. Postcard; postmarked 1910. Miniature bird stand; gilt metal with wax parrot; c1880. **P.86.** Calendar; "Pussy Cat Calendar"; 9 1/2" x 7"; 4 pp.; gilded, hanging cord, tassel; 1906. Postcard; International Art Pub., N.Y.; printed in Germany; postmarked 1907. **P.87.** Prattware pottery cats (pair); c1800. **P.88.** Children's book; 8 7/8" x 10 7/8"; *Our Pussies*; Helena Maguire, artist; Ernest Nister, London; printed in Bavaria; c1895. Postcards: c1910. Germany; postmarked France, 1902. Germany; postmarked 1908. Wilhelm Boehme, Berlin; c1900. "Unwelcome Visitors" series; "Oilette" (4-color process reproduction); Raphael Tuck & Sons, London; printed in England. A.&M.B., Germany; c1900. G.O.M., Germany; postmarked 1915. Christmas card; die-cut edge; c1895. Shaped toy booklet, "The Truants"; die cut, gilded; Lithographic Publishing, N.Y.; printed in Munich; c1895. Postcards: Embossed; Paul Finkenrath, Berlin; postmarked Belgium, 1908. T.S.N., Germany; postmarked Belgium. A.&M.B., Germany; c1910. A.&M.B., Germany; c1905. Meissner & Buch, Leipzig; c1910. Postmarked France, 1907. Raphael Tuck & Sons, London; postmarked England, 1907. Christmas card; Hildesheimer & Faulkner, London; c1895.